help & hope for the single parent

tony evans

MOODY PUBLISHERS

CHICAGO

All Scripture quotations, unless otherwise indicated, are taken from the *New American Standard Bible®*, Copyright © 1960, 1962, 1963, 1968, 1971, 1972, 1973, 1975, 1977, 1995 by The Lockman Foundation. Used by permission. (www.Lockman.org)

Interior design: Erik Peterson
Cover design: John Hamilton Design, LLC
Cover image:iStock #10770236

ISBN 978-0-8024-8942-5

We hope you enjoy this book from Moody Publishers. Our goal is to provide high-quality, thought-provoking books and products that connect truth to your real needs and challenges. For more information on other books and products written and produced from a biblical perspective, go to www.moodypublishers.com or write to:

Moody Publishers
820 N. LaSalle Boulevard
Chicago, IL 60610

1 3 5 7 9 10 8 6 4 2

Printed in the United States of America

CONTENTS

1

GOD'S VIEW OF THE SINGLE PARENT

My heart was broken recently when the son of one of the single parents in our church looked up at me and said, "Pastor, why won't God give me a dad? Every night I ask God to give me a dad, but He won't give me one."

What would you have said to him? I didn't have any easy answers for that young man, but I tried to explain to him that he did have a father, his heavenly Father. Yes, that concept may be beyond his worldview right now, but I wanted him to know that he was not alone. And I want to say to single parents that they are not alone either. Single parent, God has a word for you, and it's a word of hope and comfort.

THE NEED FOR A WORD FROM GOD

That's not to say there isn't plenty of disturbing news out there when it comes to the issue of single parents. What used to be considered rather unusual not too many years ago—a family with only one parent present —is now a crisis of growing proportions. The reality in our culture today is that a staggering number of children are growing up in single-parent homes, the vast majority of which are fatherless.

In 1970, for example, only 13 percent of children grew up without both parents being at home. But today that number is over 30 percent in the culture at large with over 21 million children being raised in a single-parent home. For African-American children, that percentage more than doubles to over 70 percent. We're talking about millions of children growing up in homes where in most cases they will know little or nothing of a father's influence. I know that mothers are leaving their families too, but the numbers are still heavily weighted toward missing fathers.

Statistics show that close to half of all American children will go through at least some part of their lives without having a father at home. The implications of this situation are staggering in terms of the world we have to live in and minister to. This is not theoretical for me. My church in Dallas is not immune to the problem. One Sunday morning I asked single parents to raise their hands; then I asked those who had been raised in a single-parent home to raise their hands. In each case a large number of people put their hands up and the problem is only getting worse.

So we need to ask, What does God have to say to single parents today? What hope and comfort does He offer to the mother who is alone and fears for her children's future because they have no father at home—and fears for herself because she has no mate? What does the Bible say to the small but growing number of fathers who are rearing children alone?

Before we turn to the Scriptures, let me say a word to the reader who may be thinking, *This is not really my problem. I'm not a single parent.* Let me say that God's Word to single parents will benefit you too, for two reasons. The first is that all Scripture is profitable. Many of the principles and truths we'll consider in this booklet will also help two-parent families in their child-rearing task. The second reason you need to know what the Word says on this issue is that you may be just one step, one heartbeat, one accident away from becoming a single parent. It could happen to any of us at any time. And as much as we hate to think about it, our homes could also be hit by divorce, death, or abandonment.

What I'm saying is that none of us is immune to the problems of life, so we need to know what God says.

Besides, even if your home stays intact you will have to deal with this issue as a Christian and a citizen of this country because the fallout of family breakup is hitting all of us. Your children may be sitting in a classroom right now where there is a high percentage of single-parent kids. And you will almost certainly come in contact with a single parent if you don't know one already. And with close to half a million children being born out of wedlock every year,[1] we're all paying a huge economic, social, and spiritual price.

GOD IS FOR THE SINGLE PARENT

So we need a word of encouragement and hope and correction from God. First of all, I want you to know that God is for the single parent. No matter how you became a single parent, if you love God and have a heart for Him, He is for you.

> GOD CAN MEET YOUR NEED. EVEN THOUGH YOU MAY NOT HAVE AN IDEAL HOME SITUATION, YOU DO HAVE AN IDEAL GOD.

In Psalm 27:10, David says, "My father and my mother have forsaken me, but the Lord will take me up." David is saying that God will be a parent when a parent is missing. God will take up the slack caused by the absent parent. That's good news. It's good to know that your child has a mother you didn't know he or she had and has a father if he or she doesn't know where the earthly father is. There is a saying I sometimes make, "If you don't have a mother, He will be your mother. If you don't have a father, He will be your Father. He will be a lawyer in a courtroom and a doctor in a hospital and whatever else you need."

God can meet your need. Even though you may not have an ideal home situation, you do have an ideal God. Filmmakers use fancy technology to turn a character in a film into someone else. God says, "If you need Me to be a father, I will be a father. If you need Me to be a mother, I will be a mother. If you need Me to be a spouse, I will be a spouse. If you need Me to be a friend, I will be a friend. I will be to you whatever you need." That's a good word for you if there is somebody important missing in your home.

David writes in the book of Psalms that God is "a father of the fatherless and a judge for the widows" (Psalm 68:5). If your child does not have a father, that's not the whole story because God is a Father to the fatherless. God also acts in justice on behalf of a widow. A widow includes those who have been abandoned by a spouse.

The Hebrew word for orphan means *fatherless*. In Israel, a fatherless child was considered an orphan even if he or she had a mother. Why? Because in the economy of God it was the job of the father to provide for and protect the family. When the father was absent, it made the family vulnerable.

In Psalm 146:9 we find more good news for single parents: "The Lord protects the strangers; He supports the fatherless and the widow; but He thwarts the way of the wicked." God supports those who are left alone. He picks up the pieces of their broken lives.

Many people who grew up in single-parent families have seen this truth in action. They made it not because their mothers had a lot to give them but because God showed up in their homes and made the difference. He made a way when there seemed to be no way. He provided when there seemed to be no provision. The fact is, God is so much for the single parent and the child with no dad that it could literally cost someone his life to abuse them:

> You shall not afflict any widow or orphan. If you afflict him at all, and if he does cry out to Me, I will surely hear his cry; and My anger will be kindled, and I will kill you with the sword; and your wives shall become widows and your children fatherless. (Exodus 22:22–24)

God says that you should treat single parents well because to do otherwise is to place yourself only one step away from that condition yourself. If you are a single parent, this should help you to see how valuable you are. If God will go to your defense at such an extreme level, then you should take comfort in His great love for you.

> YET GOD TAKES SPECIAL CARE TO MENTION HIS GREAT LOVE FOR THOSE WHO ARE VULNERABLE AND ALONE IN TRYING TO RAISE A FAMILY.

Let me show you one more passage by way of introduction and setting the stage—one more word that shows God's love and care for the single-parent family:

> At the end of every third year you shall bring out all the tithe of your produce in that year, and shall deposit it in your town. And the Levite, because he has no portion or inheritance among you, and the alien, the orphan and the widow who are in your town, shall come and eat and be satisfied, in order that the Lord your God may bless you in all the work of your hand which you do. (Deuteronomy 14:28–29)

In other words, how you treat the fatherless family will often determine how your Father in heaven treats you. How you relate to people who are in need will affect God's hand of goodness on you. One of the worst things you can do is to spurn people who have not had the opportunities and privileges you have had; we can't know how someone ended up in the situation they are in without having walked in their shoes.

It is easy for you as a single parent to feel less valuable than those who come from a nuclear family. Or perhaps you feel out of place when you compare yourself to other families, or you feel like you are something less worthy or important than they are. Yet God takes special care to mention His great love for those who are vulnerable and alone in trying to raise a family.

These passages will give you an idea of how God feels about single parents and their children. But now I want to get very specific and give hope to the single parent who works hard each and every day to make a living for themselves and their children, then has to come home and make dinner, wash clothes, help with the homework, only to go to bed alone at night—then do it all over again the next day, with no one there to turn to for help, comfort, companionship and guidance. For those of you who are single parents, you've got a kindred spirit in Hagar.

THE SAGA OF HAGAR

I call the story of Hagar a saga because it has all the elements of a great drama, and it has some real-life lessons in it for us as well. We first meet Hagar in Genesis 16, where we learn that she was the servant of Sarai, and that Sarai and Abram (this was just before their names were changed) were unable to have children.

It was the custom of the day in situations like this to bring in another woman who would bear the husband's child and thus act as a surrogate for the barren wife. This was the case with Hagar—Sarai proposed the plan to Abram, who followed her advice.

Now it's obvious that Sarai wanted a child desperately. But we also need to remember that God had promised her that she would bear a child someday. The promise hadn't been fulfilled yet, so, like many of us, Sarai decided to help God out. By her actions she was saying, "Lord, I know Your intentions are good, but since You can't pull this off, let me help You."

Sarai gave Hagar to Abram, and Abram went into Hagar's tent for the purpose of conceiving a child (v. 4). Bad idea. It was doomed from the start because it was an attempt to bypass God's method and timing and force Him to fulfill His promise.

It was also a bad idea on the human level because it backfired. When Hagar got pregnant, she evidently began to look down on Sarai, and this made Sarai feel hurt and jealous. Even though the whole thing was her idea, she said to Abram, "That woman is not staying around here." So in verses 5–6 Abram and Sarai have an argument about Hagar and Abram backs down from taking any initiative in the issue. He tells her, "Do whatever you want. I'm staying out of this one."

Before we move on, I just want to remind you that it is never a good idea to try and help God out. If God did not ask for your help, don't assume that He needs it. God has a way to accomplish what He has promised, and so when we try to "help" God – it only makes the situation worse. It reveals that we lack faith. Abram and Sarai wanted to help God out, but all they did was create larger problems between Ishmael's and Isaac's descendants that have lasted for generations, even until this day.

Sarai drove Hagar out of the house, and suddenly she found herself alone and pregnant, with no Abram or any other male to support and protect her. She was about to become a single parent because she got caught in someone else's plan to help God. A lot of single parents didn't ask for their status. It was brought upon them by someone else's decisions or disobedience, or possibly someone else's persuasion or pressure. But I like verses 7–10 of Genesis 16:

> Now the angel of the Lord found her by a spring of water in the wilderness, by the spring on the way to Shur. And he said, "Hagar, Sarai's maid, where have you come from and where are you going?" And she said, "I am fleeing from the presence of my mistress Sarai." Then the angel of the Lord said to her, "Return to your mistress, and submit yourself to her authority." Moreover, the angel of the Lord said to her, "I will greatly multiply your descendants so that they shall be too many to count."

The star of the saga arrives: the Angel of the Lord. Notice how often this title is repeated in just these few verses that it was the Angel of the Lord who found Hagar. That's good news when you have been rejected. That's good news when the father of your child is nowhere to be found. That's good news when you find yourself alone and vulnerable.

Who is the Angel of the Lord? The Old Testament indicates that He was the revelation of God's presence. Later on, when Abraham was about to sacrifice Isaac, the son he and Sarah had waited for all those years, it was the Angel of the Lord who stopped him and said, "Now I know that you fear God, since you have not withheld your son, your only son, from Me" (Genesis 22:12). The

Angel of the Lord speaks as though He is God, yet He is distinct from God the Father. Who then is this divine person who finds Hagar in the wilderness? He is Jesus Christ before His incarnation in Bethlehem.

The Angel of the Lord is the preincarnate Son of God. He is the eternal second person of the Godhead. He did not show up for the first time as baby Jesus in a manger in Bethlehem—there is no time when Jesus did not exist. He has always existed and He made His appearance throughout the Old Testament as the Angel of the Lord.

What does the Angel of the Lord do? He shows up to make things better. Isn't that just like Jesus? He shows up in the Old Testament and in the New Testament. How can He do that? Because He is the same yesterday, today, and forever (Hebrews 13:8). The preincarnate Christ went out to the wilderness for the benefit of a single mother-to-be.

First of all, He found her. If you are a single parent, God knows where you are, the situation you are in, and how you got into the struggles that you now face. He loves you, forgives you for wrong choices you may have made, and shows great compassion on you. When you hurt, He feels it. He knows your loneliness, stigma, and pain. After all, He experienced the fullness of all three on the cross.

The Lord told Hagar in verse 11 that He was very much aware of her condition and very much involved in and interested in the birth of her son. Keep in mind, that

even though the situation in which the child was con-
ceived may have been less than ideal, in order for that
child to be formed in the mother's womb, God had to go
to work.

Sometimes we talk about the relationship that produced a child as illegitimate because it was outside the
bonds of marriage. But there is no such thing as an illegitimate child, because God has never had a baby that
was not legitimate. That is, God has never made a mistake
in giving a baby to a set of parents; it is never the case
that He didn't mean for that child to be there or consid-
ers that child to be any less than a fully valuable human
being.

I say that because God's response to the conception
and birth of Ishmael is a strong reminder that every child
is special. The Bible says in Psalm 139 that every baby is
woven together in the womb by God. Whatever the circumstances of a child's conception, the child produced
by that relationship is legitimate because that child bears
the image of God.

That ought to be good news for single parents. It does
not justify wrong actions, but it is an affirmation that God
recognizes the value of each life. Not only did God rec-
ognize the life of Hagar's child, but He named the baby
"Ishmael" (Genesis 16:11). The Hebrew word for this
means "God hears." In other words, God knows what I am
going through. Guess what, single parent? God knows.
He knows the trouble and stress that you are in, and He
knows whether it's a situation you got yourself into, some-

one else put you in, or whether it is a mixture of both. He also knows where you are right at this very moment.

God showed up in the wilderness and told Hagar what to name her baby. Why is that good? Because every time she ran out of diapers she could say, "Ishmael needs diapers," for she knew that God was listening. When she didn't have enough food to feed Ishmael, his name reminded her that God knew that she needed food for her baby. The value of the child is also reflected in the fact that God described details about his future life and personality (v. 12).

Single parent, God knows what you and your children need. The reason God gave Ishmael his name was so that every time Hagar used that name, she would remember something about God. The Angel of the Lord told her to call him Ishmael so that every time she spoke his name she would remember "God hears and God knows."

That's the beauty of the grace of God for a single parent. Hagar is out on her own with no help, but God says, "I know." He goes on to say in verse 11 that she would have a son and that they would be all right "because the Lord has given heed to your affliction" (v. 11).

Now notice verse 13: "Then she called the name of the Lord who spoke to her, 'You are a God who sees.'" The Hebrew word for the name Hagar gave to God is El Roi. El Roi simply means that God sees. Do you know that God sees? He sees the circumstances you are in. He sees you out there in the desert all alone with no one to provide for you, give you spiritual and emotional covering, and protect you. He is not unaware of what you are going through. No matter what your family situation may be, no matter what your need or loss, God says, "I see. I hear. I know."

Verse 15 records the birth of Ishmael and his naming by Abram, under God's direction. Now every time Abram called Ishmael by name, he too would be reminded of the trouble he had made. He would remember, "God knows the situation I have created."

The Angel of the Lord showed up in a bad situation, but the saga of Hagar does not end here. Turn over to Genesis 21 and look at the conclusion of the story. Hagar has gone back to Sarah, as the Lord told her to do. And by now Sarah has had Isaac, the son of promise whom she and Abraham (their names were changed in chapter 17) were waiting for all along.

Both mothers and their sons were living in the same tent. And there was trouble. Sarah saw Ishmael making fun of Isaac, the son of promise (v. 9). She did not like that at all. Ishmael was a teenager now. Teenagers will do that. But Sarah said, "Not in my house you won't!"

Abraham didn't like this mess any better than he did the first one, but Sarah demanded that he give Hagar her marching papers. Abraham was very distressed, but God assured him that He was in control and that He would personally care for Hagar and Ishmael (v. 12). So according to verse 14, Abraham sent Hagar and Ishmael away from his house to wander in the wilderness alone. Hagar was now a bona fide single mother.

Soon the water Abraham gave to her and the boy was used up, and she left him so that she wouldn't have to watch him die (vv. 15–16). But the Angel of God (Jesus, before His birth in Bethlehem) showed up again, assuring Hagar that God knew exactly what was happening and would not only keep her and Ishmael alive but would make a great nation out of him (vv. 17–18).

This is a classic single-parent scenario—one that, with a few changes of detail and geography, could easily be repeated today. Hagar lost her home, she had a teenage son to take care of, and she was on the streets, so to speak, with no money in her pockets. She was thirsty and probably hungry. She feared that her boy would die. So in despair she sat down and cried.

That's when the Son of God showed up in His Old Testament form. He asked Hagar, "What is the matter with you?" (v. 17). Didn't He know the mess she was in? Of course He did. He was saying, "Hagar, have you forgotten what I did for you earlier? Have you forgotten how I found you out in the wilderness when you were pregnant and Sarah had chased you away? Do you think I am going to remember you one minute and forget you the next? You yourself said I am the God who sees. Do you think that now I have gone blind?"

Single parent, God has not gone blind. He sees, He hears, and He knows. You may be in a far from ideal situation, but you have an ideal God. You have got a God who, when your husband and the father of your baby forces you out of the home, will turn into a husband, if necessary, and be a Father to your child or children. God will always provide.

Why? Because His name is El Roi, "the God who sees." He is the way out of your lonely and negative circumstances. Now I can't promise you that He will bring you a mate or a home or anything on your wish list. But I can tell you that He sees you and your child or children, and He hears your cry. He says, "Remember, I named Ishmael. And any child who has My name, I am going to take care of."

That is the beauty of dedicating children to the Lord—you give that child to God. And when you give that child to God, God takes responsibility for that child's well-being. So God's message to Hagar was, "Have you forgotten who I am?"

Genesis 21:18–21, the final chapter of this biblical saga, shows how God fulfilled His word. The well Hagar saw in verse 19 was there all the time, but she was so consumed with sadness and crying and forgetting God that she stopped trusting, she stopped looking for God.

> THE GREATEST THING A SINGLE PARENT CAN DO IS TO HAVE A PASSION FOR GOD.

How many times has God opened your eyes and shown you a well, a source of supply, when you did not see any way, with no husband, that you would be able to make it? How many times has God opened your eyes and shown you how you can make it on one person's salary alone?

A sister in our church who is a single parent once came to see me. Her whole world had collapsed. She said she just did not see a way, so we called on God together. I got a call two days later. "Let me tell you what Jesus did," she began, and she went on to tell me how Jesus had made a way. I wasn't surprised. He is the Angel of the Lord. He knows where you are. He is the God who sees you.

The greatest thing a single parent can do is to have a passion for God, because when you have a passion for God you have Someone who can be a Father to your child and be a Husband, a protector, to you. Single father, when you know God you have Someone to lean on who understands a father's heart and a father's desires for his children. He is the God who sees and knows and cares.

This was brought home forcefully in my own home a long time ago when my daughter Chrystal was not yet married. My daughter Chrystal's life revolves around a schedule notebook she carries. She keeps all her plans and papers and credit cards and a lot of other important things in this notebook. One day she inadvertently put it on top of her car and then drove off, forgetting it was on the roof. She got home and discovered that it was gone. She remembered what she had done and drove back over to the mall to look for it. But her notebook was nowhere to be found. She came back home crying.

As she sat there shedding tears, she began flipping through her daily calendar. She came to one of the verses and read this statement under it: "God will be a husband to you if you need one."

Chrystal looked at that statement and prayed, "God, You said You would be a husband to someone who needs one. I need you to be a husband to me right now and find this book that has my life in it."

When she had said that, the telephone rang. A man asked, "Is this Chrystal Evans?" She said it was. He explained that he was driving down the street when he saw something that looked like a book lying alongside the road. He thought it looked important, so he doubled back and picked it up.

He brought it home and saw Chrystal's name in it. "I live fifty miles from there," he went on. "I just happened to be in that neighborhood today. I wanted to know if I can bring you your notebook tomorrow morning."

I want you to know we had church in the Evans house that night. We had church because even though Chrystal did not know where her notebook was, El Roi, "the God who sees," knew where it was. He came through at just the right time. I went with her to pick up the notebook and meet the man. He said, "By the way, I'm a Christian." God can make a way where there seems to be no way. God says He will never leave you by yourself.

Now, I know someone will say that was luck. Others will say it happened just by chance. But there is going to come a day when you will lose more than a notebook, and on that day you will need to know who Jesus is. He is the Angel of the Lord, "the God who sees." That is the message here. If you are not in an ideal situation, God is here to make up the difference. Hagar, don't just sit there crying. Call on the name of the Lord. He will hear you.

> Be strong and courageous, do not be afraid or tremble at them, for the Lord your God is the one who goes with you. He will not fail you or forsake you. (Deuteronomy 31:6)

God says that He is never going to leave you out there by yourself. But the context says that this promise is to those who live lives that honor Him. If you are living faithfully to please God, whatever your marital or financial circumstance, if you are holding on to God as your priority, then you have His promise that He will never leave you or forsake you.

Note

1. http://www.fas.org/sgp/crs/misc/RS20301.pdf

2

YOUR VIEW OF
SINGLE PARENTING

Many of us don't feel that God is near because we have forsaken Him by the way we live. Then we wonder why we don't see Him present in our circumstances. God says that, if we will commit ourselves to live for Him, He will be present with us in our circumstances. A single parent might say, "But Jesus doesn't understand my situation." Yes, He does, in at least two important ways.

First, on the night He was crucified, Jesus was totally abandoned, left alone by everyone. No single parent or any other person has ever been abandoned by other humans as completely as Jesus was abandoned. Yet on that night He said, "I am not alone, because the Father is with Me" (John 16:32). Jesus experienced the presence of God the Father on the night of His abandonment, and so can you.

Jesus also understands your situation because we can presume that sometime before the crucifixion, Joseph, His earthly father had died. While He was on the cross, Jesus told John to care for Mary as his own mother because Jesus would no longer be able to provide for her (John 19:26–27). He wouldn't have done that if Joseph had still been around. So for some portion of Jesus' life, He was the son of a single parent.

Jesus knows exactly what you are going through, and that is why in Luke 7:11–17, when Jesus encountered the widow of Nain on her way to bury her son, He sympathized with her and raised her son from the dead. That is why Hebrews 4:15 says that as our High Priest Jesus feels what you feel. He knows what you are going through because He has been there. He not only can help you, but He can share the feelings you have while He is helping you.

> IT IS BETTER TO BE FAITHFUL TO GOD AND NOT TO HAVE A HUSBAND THAN TO HAVE TO LEAVE GOD BEHIND JUST TO HAVE A MATE.

God the Father can know what you are going through because He is God. But God the Father can't feel what you are going through because He has never been a man. However, because Jesus has experienced everything you and I have experienced and felt everything we have felt, He can say, "I fully understand what you're going through." When Jesus the Son goes before the Father on your behalf as your High Priest and the Holy Spirit interprets your most deeply felt prayers to the Father (Romans 8:26), you get the ministry of the entire Trinity working in your situation. You get the total provision of God for your circumstances.

THE LESSON OF RUTH

I believe that every single mother, if not every woman regardless of her circumstances, should make a habit of reading the story of Ruth. Ruth is an extraordinary example of a faithful woman with some incredible lessons to teach us.

She was not an Israelite, as we learn right off. Her mother-in-law Naomi was, but she was living in Ruth's country of Moab because there was a famine in her hometown of Bethlehem. When Naomi's husband and her two sons died, she took Ruth in as her own. When Naomi decided to return to Bethlehem, she tried to persuade Ruth to go back to her father's home and find a nice Moabite man to marry. However, Ruth said she would rather be alone with Naomi and her people and the true God than find a new husband in the wrong group of people.

Single parent, did you notice that? It is better to be faithful to God and not to have a husband than to have to leave God behind just to have a mate. This truth is just as applicable to single fathers and widowers.

Ruth was ready to give up the thought of ever marrying again if that's what it took to be a follower of God.

Naomi warned Ruth that her marriage prospects in Bethlehem would be absolutely none. But to Ruth there was
something more important than having a man beside her
at night.

Chances are you know how the story of Ruth ends.
She meets Boaz and not only marries him but, in the
process, becomes a part of the lineage of David and even-
tually of Jesus Himself. Naomi didn't have the whole pic-
ture in front of her. God honored Ruth's faithfulness in a
way neither woman could have guessed. Now you may
say, "That's great, Tony. Nice, happy ending. But I'm not
Ruth, and this is not Bethlehem. I'm fifty-one years old
and I doubt there is a Boaz for me any longer."

Maybe not, but your God is the God of Ruth. Of
course, I can't say whether, or when, or even if, God will
give you a new mate. He doesn't share that kind of information with me. But He sees and knows you. He's watch-
ing and listening. He knows the deepest desires and needs
of your heart. And He is your husband if or until you have
one on earth.

If Ruth were here, she would tell you it's worth it to be
faithful to the Lord. She became part of the godly line
because she was willing to go all the way with God in her
single state.

YOUR VIEW OF YOU

Now I want to turn to a crucial area, which is the system God has put in place to help us deal with situations

such as single-parent families and single women in particular who have no one to care for them. God has given all of us spheres of responsibility. Our marital or family status does not excuse us from carrying out our God-assigned responsibilities, because in His economy, or way of ordering life, God always starts with personal responsibility. So the first question we always need to ask ourselves is: What is my responsibility under God? Once we understand that, we can move out in concentric circles to the broader contexts of the responsibilities God has assigned to the family, the church, and society.

Before I get to the responsibilities of the single parent, a couple of general observations will help us understand why it seems that so little of what God wants done in this world actually gets done. The problem comes when we flip-flop roles, when we blur and mix the circles of responsibility God has clearly drawn and mess up His order. God never expects your family to do for you what you ought to be doing for yourself. God never expects the church to do for you what your family should be doing for you. And God never expects society to do the job of the church.

Today we have it all mixed up, all out of order, with the result of things having been made worse not better. We have too many people who want society and the government to do for them what they are not willing to do for themselves. We have people who expect the church to do for them what ought to be the responsibility of their families. So we get the system out of order. When that happens, we end up with the chaos we have in the whole welfare system. We end up with children who have no sense of responsibility toward their parents, even though in some cases their parents have invested years in taking care of grown children who should have left home a long time ago. (This is not to say that at times grown children, for various reasons, may still be in their parents' home or may have to return temporarily.) We're in the mess we're in because we are operating outside of God's system. We've got to get back in sync with Him or else nothing will work.

It is important that we do not let others make us feel guilty for staying in sync with God's economy. What many people will do is make you feel guilty that you are not doing for them what they ought to be doing for themselves. If you don't watch out, you'll wind up feeling bad and they'll wind up feeling good, when it ought to be the other way around. A lot of parents of single parents feel guilty because their son or daughter is having to rear children alone. But a lot of that guilt is false guilt. Parents cannot make their grown children's decisions for them, and sometimes each us makes poor decisions.

So what is the responsibility of single parents? What must they do? What does God expect of them? I want to answer that from Scripture by looking with you at the story of a widow in 1 Kings 17:9–24.

This account shows us that, if you are alone and without the support systems you need, if you are financially destitute and see very little hope of making it, the first thing you must do as a single parent is to obey God. You may say, "I want something practical. You're giving me theology." Well, this theology is extremely practical. Just ask the widow at Zarephath. Here was a woman with a son to feed who had run out of the means by which to live. She was destitute.

In fact, she had only enough oil and flour for one more meal, yet God sent her a boarder, the prophet Elijah. Notice that God told Elijah, "I have commanded [her] to provide for you" (v. 9). So this woman was about to be confronted with the issue of obedience to God—and, by the way, she wasn't even an Israelite.

One thing you need to know right off is that if you trust God it does not matter what race, class, or creed you are—He will take care of you. He sent Elijah to a Gentile woman and told the prophet He had already put it in her heart to feed him because there was a famine and the prophet needed to eat.

So Elijah came to this single parent and asked for a meal. The widow told him her plight, that she was planning a last meal for herself and her son because of the famine (v. 12). She was saying, "I don't see any way out." I have sat with single parents who have said the same thing. I think any single parent can understand how this woman must have felt. Her statement was not in conflict with God's desire for her, because at this point she is simply stating the reality. Her obedience hasn't been tested yet. She didn't have much, but Elijah asked for it anyway because he knew what God was going to do.

This woman faced a big question, one that many single parents face today: Do I obey God even though I am a single parent who has very little to offer? Or do I take the little that I have and keep it for myself? She did have the promise of God to act on, for Elijah told her:

> Do not fear; go, do as you have said, but make me a little bread cake from it first, and bring it out to me, and afterward you may make one for yourself and for your son. For thus says the Lord God of Israel, "The bowl of flour shall not be exhausted, nor shall the jar of oil be empty, until the day that the Lord sends rain on the face of the earth." (vv. 13–14)

Here is the classic dilemma for people of faith, single parent or not. Are we going to obey God and get His long-term blessing, or are we going to disobey Him in order to get a short-term fix? A lot of us will settle for the latter because we have a hard time seeing with the eyes of faith. This may be even a bigger temptation for single-parent families, since the short-term prospects often do not look good and it seems unwise to risk what little they have.

> GOD WANTS US TO LEARN TO OPERATE ON HIS WORD AND NOT ON OUR CIRCUMSTANCES.

This Gentile widow could have said no to Elijah and eaten her last meal. But she had a heart that was open to the God of Israel, and she acted on His Word, not on her situation. Single parent, if all you see is your present situation, you are going to be controlled by it. What God wants you—and all of us, for that matter—to do, is to learn to operate on His Word and not on our circumstances. I once asked a single mother how she was doing, and she said, "Okay, under the circumstances." Get out from under there. You don't belong under the circumstances. What God wants you to do is to step out on His Word.

Now please don't misunderstand. I am very much aware of the burdens single parents carry, and I am not into handing out easy answers. But what I'm talking about is real-world Christian living. I saw a practical example of what happens when we act on God's Word. Another of the single parents in our church, who was concerned about her giving, came to me. Things were tight, but she wanted to honor the Lord. So we prayed about it, and I told her, "Well, just honor God with what you can."

We talked awhile longer and she left. Soon after that she called to tell me about somebody who had died in her family and left her a large inheritance. Now I know what you're thinking! But I am not going to tell you that if you give faithfully God is going to take out somebody in your family and dump a big inheritance on you. What I am saying is that this single mother honored God in her situation, and He honored her heart toward Him. She had a heart that wanted to obey God.

The widow of Zarephath also had a heart to obey

God, and we read in 1 Kings 17:15–16 how God kept His promise made to her by Elijah. She and her son not only did not die but "ate for many days." She didn't get a big inheritance, but God kept her jar and bowl filled with enough flour and oil for each day's need. That may be how He honors your obedience. The point is that God gave her what she did not have because she obeyed what God said. Before you complain about what God is not doing for you, your first question must be, "Am I doing what He told me to do?"

If you are not obeying God, then don't be surprised if you are not eating for many days. God's ability to supply is never the issue. Paul writes, "Now to Him who is able to do far more abundantly beyond all that we ask or think, according to the power that works within us" (Ephesians 3:20). The power is working in us when we obey. The issue is our obedience to the Word of God.

By the way, this widow was not a perfect single parent. Go on further to 1 Kings 17:17–18 and you find that her son died and she feared that it was God punishing her for her sins. In other words, she had some bad things in her past, some mistakes she had made, some sins she had committed, some not-so-nice circumstances, things she would rather forget. She was not a perfect person, but that's the beauty of God's grace. If you have an imperfect background but you are willing to obey God today, He can take care of the miracles you need tomorrow. If you have an imperfect past but an obedient present, you can have a blessed tomorrow.

This woman obeyed, and she saw yet another miracle when Elijah raised her son from the dead. Her story ought to be good news for any single parent. Yesterday's sins don't have to cancel tomorrow's blessings. If you will obey God today, if you have put yesterday's sins under the blood of Jesus and are not repeating them today, God wants to bless you based on your obedience.

3

HOW OTHERS
ARE TO VIEW
THE SINGLE PARENT

Another place in Scripture where we see the principle of God's provision in a time of need for a single parent is found in 2 Kings. This time God's prophet is Elisha, and the woman in the story is another destitute widow (2 Kings 4:1–7). Her husband had been one of the "sons of the prophets" (v. 1), so he was a godly man. The woman herself said that about him. But she was about to lose her children because she couldn't pay her debts and her creditors were at the door. A lot of single parents can identify with this scenario because the financial burdens of single parenthood can sometimes make you feel like you and your kids have been sold into slavery. There is a direct correlation between increase in poverty and single parenting.

Notice how differently God dealt with this situation. Remember the single mother who wanted to honor God by giving what she could and she received a large inheritance? That's the kind of solution God uses here. Whereas the widow of Zarephath apparently got just enough food supply to last each day, this woman got a windfall of oil, enough to pay off all her debts and set her and her sons up for life.

You can read the story for yourself. The point is that, when Elisha asked the woman what she had, she told him her circumstances, just like the other widow did with Elijah. But like Elijah, Elisha then took her a step beyond that and challenged her to live by faith. For this widow the moment of truth came when Elisha told her to get as many vessels as she could lay her hands on. She could have looked at the reality of the situation and said, "Borrow vessels? For what? I don't have anything to pour in them." Or she could live by faith.

She made the right choice. Living by faith meant going to every person in the neighborhood and getting every empty vessel she could, because she didn't know how the Lord was going to do it and when He was going to do it, but she believed He was going to meet the need.

Once you are convinced that God is able and that your circumstances are not the ultimate determination of God's ability, then you're ready to act in faith. We tend to focus on the wrong thing. We focus on how bad things are with us, not on how great things are with Him.

Philippians 4:19 says that God will supply all your

needs "according to His riches," not according to your circumstances. Satan keeps us focused so much on our inability rather than on God's ability that we rarely see the great "over and above" supply of God.

Here we have two single mothers who saw God do more for them than what they had in the house to work with. Again, the issue is not what you have. It is what God has. All He asked those widows to do was obey Him; He took responsibility for the supply.

Did you know that Paul's spiritual son Timothy was the product of a single-parent home, as far as we can determine? If Timothy's father was not physically absent, he was at least spiritually absent, for the faith Timothy had was the result of his godly mother and grandmother (2 Timothy 1:5). Timothy was influenced by Eunice and Lois, and he turned out to be a man of God. Even if there is not a godly man in your home, God can take up the slack.

> IF YOU WILL OBEY GOD AS A SINGLE PARENT, LIVE BY FAITH, AND GENERATE AS MUCH GODLY INFLUENCE AS YOU ARE ABLE, YOU CAN TRUST THE REST TO GOD.

How could Timothy become a man of God when he did not have a male influence in his life? Because he had two women who knew how to get hold of the best male in the universe—the heavenly Father.

Many of us are Christians today not because we had

a great male model in our lives but because we had a
mother or grandmother or aunt who knew a great God.
She made us go to Sunday school and church when we
did not want to go. And God was able to catch hold of
what she planted and bring about a transformation in our
lives.

Don't be upset that you can't be a mother and a father. God does not expect you to be both a mother and a
father. He expects you to be the best mother you can be.
He will take care of being a father if you will be a mother
who is obedient and faithful to Him.

Timothy was not perfect either. He had some timid-
ity. He had some fears. But at the right time God gave
Timothy a Paul, a godly father figure and example, somebody who would give the male influence he needed at the
time he needed it. If you will obey God as a single parent,
live by faith, and generate as much godly influence as you
are able, you can trust the rest to God. All He asks of you
is to fulfill your personal responsibility.

FAMILY

What about the family of the single parent? I would
say there's a good chance that you have a single parent
somewhere in your extended family. The statistics alone
make that a pretty safe assumption. Scripture has a lot to
say about the responsibility a family bears to its single
parents and widows.

The Old Testament had a number of options for taking

care of a widow. One option was for her to marry a relative of her husband to keep the family intact; a second option was for her son to take care of her if he was old enough to do so. A third option was for her to go back home to live with her father. In the New Testament, Paul writes,

> If any widow has children or grandchildren, they must first learn to practice piety in regard to their own family and to make some return to their parents; for this is acceptable in the sight of God. . . . But if anyone does not provide for his own, and especially for those of his household, he has denied the faith and is worse than an unbeliever. . . . If any woman who is a believer has dependent widows, she must assist them and the church must not be burdened, so that it may assist those who are widows indeed. (1 Timothy 5:4, 8, 16)

The point is inescapable. The next line of defense, protection, and support for the single-parent family, particularly if the parent is a woman, is the family of that single parent. It is not the church, nor is it the government. In fact, Paul says specifically not to burden the church with the care of someone who has family to take care of her. Why? Because children are to "make some return to their parents" (v. 4).

Some of us believers ought to be ashamed of the way we treat our parents. I grant that they were not perfect. I grant that they made mistakes. But nobody else has invested in you the amount of years, time, money, attention, pain, frustration, aggravation, irritation, and love that your parents did.

If you have neglected your parents, who have made such an investment in your life, according to Paul you rank below the worst of sinners (1 Timothy 5:8). He says that even atheists do better than that. Even people who don't know God will take care of their parents.

Some people get upset if the church or the government does not take care of their parents. But your parents did not rear the church or the government. Your parents reared you, and, if God has blessed and honored you, then you need to see to their well-being.

We often read about athletes who make it to the pros and get the big contracts. Many times they will say that the first thing they are going to do with the money is to build their mothers a house. They are on the right track.

What they are saying to their mothers is, "You hung in there with me. You did not forsake me. You did not throw me away. So because you stayed in there with me, I want to honor you. It's payback time, Mom."

Some of us need to go today, pick up the telephone, and apologize to our parents because we rarely call or check into their welfare. Someone may say, "But you don't know what my parents did to me!" Yes, some parents were far from ideal. Yet, even if they were not perfect, you still have a responsibility to them. It's an even greater responsibility if you have a single parent to care for.

What about younger single parents who are still trying to rear their children alone? If they are doing all they can and still need help, they should be able to turn to their families before they turn to the church or the government.

I know that's not popular, but it's biblical. If a single parent has to go to the church or to the welfare office and say, "I need help, but my family turned me down," that's a shame to the family. We need to care for those in our household (v. 8).

The Church

The church's responsibility to single parents and older widows is outlined in 1 Timothy 5:16. Here we run into the phrase "widows indeed." These are widows who have no one to support them. They are out there by themselves. For these women, the next line of defense is the church. The church is an extended family. That's how God meant the church to be viewed. The Greek word for church means a "called-out people." In the New Testament, "church" always referred to people not buildings.

In fact, Paul told Timothy to treat the people in the church as his fathers and mothers and brothers and sisters (1 Timothy 5:1–2). We call each other brothers and sisters in Christ because God views the church as an extension of our family. It is God's family, and He is the Father. Jesus Christ is also called our elder brother. These relationships are especially important when it comes to caring for single parents and their children, because it helps us to understand that when God talks about the church He is referring to His family.

You get the idea. The church gathers on Sunday and then it scatters, but it never quits being the church, just like a family doesn't stop being a family just because the members scatter to school and work in the morning. That's why Paul can tell the church to care for its single parents and widows who are alone: because the church is to function every day.

> IT IS IMPORTANT TO SEE HOW GOD DESIGNED THE CHURCH TO FUNCTION AS A FAMILY FOR THOSE WHO DON'T HAVE AN IMMEDIATE FAMILY TO FALL BACK ON FOR HELP AND SUPPORT.

It is important to see how God designed the church to function as a family for those who don't have an immediate family to fall back on for help and support. The book of James is called a general epistle, but we know that the author was writing to an assembly of believers because of what he said in James 2:2—the context is the church. Now go back to 1:27: "Pure and undefiled religion in the sight of our God and Father is this [in this family relationship]: to visit orphans and widows in their distress, and to keep oneself unstained by the world."

God says that your relationship to the single-parent family determines how truly Christian you are. The issue is not how you treat the rich and famous but how you treat those who are in distress, the ones Jesus called the "least" of His brothers (Matthew 25:40). These are the people who don't have any reputation, recognition, or esteem. It is what you do for them that reveals how deeply your religion has penetrated your heart.

So the church has the responsibility to care for the orphan and the widow as part of God's extended family. Such care is to be done in an accountable and responsible way so as to increase personal responsibility and not an entitlement of long-term dependency. We are the ones who are to provide the support mechanism for those people who need it. That is why the social service ministry at our church in Dallas is so comprehensive and is expanding all the time. Whether it is helping someone with job training or skill development, helping a person get an equivalent to a high school education, or providing food and clothing for more immediate needs, we are committed to taking care of those in need in our assembly, and as much as possible, even to those beyond (Galatians 6:10).

Another important ministry we are thoroughly committed to is providing spiritual role models for those who are missing them at home. We have men investing their time in boys who don't have fathers. We have spiritual mentoring taking place on a number of levels because we believe it is vital for the church as an extended family to take up the slack. One practical way God becomes a father to the fatherless and a mother to the motherless is providing surrogate parents through either spiritual men or women in the church.

I believe that mentoring should exist for both the single parent and the child through "ministry in" and "ministry out." For "ministry in," parents should find someone who understands their specific needs and who prays, counsels, listens to, and spends time with them. It helps if mothers find other women and if fathers find other men to serve this function. At some point, the single parent may well have gone through relational difficulties. As he or she begins to heal and become healthy, she (or he) should "minister out" by becoming a mentor to someone else. That does not mean that she ceases to be mentored herself. When a single parent helps others who are new to single parenting or to spiritual things in general, she aids her own healing and growth.

I encourage single parents to start this process by asking themselves what they want from a mentor, then to seek help from friends, teachers, service organizations, or other resources. And I strongly encourage single parents to challenge their church to start a mentoring program.

This kind of ministry, or the lack of it, tells you what kind of church you are in. The effectiveness of your church and mine is not measured by the size of the building we can put up, the number of people we can pack in the pews or the amount of the offering we can take in on a Sunday morning. It is not measured by how popular the choir is or how many radio stations the pastor is on.

The church is measured, according to James, by how much attention is being given to the least among us, to the people who have no base, no family support. If caring for them is not a priority in the church, then James says our religion is worthless. If all we do is cater to the "up and in," to people who can do something for us in return, then James says we have missed the essence of the Christian faith. Many of us have worthless religion because we don't have time to use the blessings God has given us to help somebody in distress. James says that orphans and widows are at the top of that list. By and large, they are the single-parent family.

The church should position itself to provide financial counseling to those who need it, the opportunity for someone who needs it to pursue a GED or receive training toward getting their GED, skills development training, and the like to better equip singles in order to support themselves.

Another thing the church must do is to hold the biological family accountable as the first line of defense. We saw in 1 Timothy 5:16 that Paul told Timothy to tell the families in the church at Ephesus what their duties were so that the church would not be burdened with the care of those who had family members available to help meet their needs. So the first thing we in the church must do is make sure that families are being families.

We are living in a world where family members don't want to be responsible for each other. They don't want to be families anymore. They don't want the responsibility. It's hard holding a family together today. But the church needs to call families to shoulder their responsibilities so that the church can be free to assist those who are out there all alone with nobody to help.

THE GOVERNMENT

The final concentric circle in God's structure of responsibility for single parents is society, the government. Single parent, the government is last, not first. You don't go for a welfare check first.

I am not playing politics now. I am not talking about whether you are a Democrat or a Republican. I am talking about whether you are biblical. You don't go to the government first. You don't find out what Uncle Sam has for you before you have dealt with the prior areas of responsibility and help.

The first thing you find out is what God has for you. You go to His Word. After that, you find out what support systems are in your nuclear or extended family. Then, you go to the family of God. When all else fails, that is when the broader society helps out. I must say again that we've mixed God's order all up. We have a generation today that has been trained to go to the government first.

> **IF YOU HAVE NOT STARTED WITH GOD, YOU HAVE STARTED WRONG.**

In fact, they go to the government before they even fulfill their personal responsibilities. If a person is unwilling to fulfill his or her responsibilities, no one else should help him (2 Thessalonians 3:10).

Then they become angry if the government does not meet their needs. So they go to the church for help, and if that doesn't do the job, they turn to their family and get mad if a brother or sister or some other family member doesn't want to step in and help.

My message to that person is, you started at the wrong place. If you have not started with God, you have started wrong. The government is your last line of defense. Romans 13:1–4 says that the job of the government is to make sure order and justice are maintained so that we can conduct our lives without fear of chaos. God did not ordain government to set up and administer these massive giveaway entitlement programs.

This hits home, particularly for those of us who are of African-American descent. Back in the days of slavery, there were no government programs, no societal support, and no federal grants. Yet families took care of each other. It goes back to the family connection, where everybody was related to everybody else. If you did not have a father, the man down the street became your father. If you did not have a mother, the woman up the street became your mother. And if there was nobody to be found for you in your family or in the neighborhood, there was always somebody at church who would love you. That is how it is supposed to be.

If we want to reverse our single-parent crisis, we have to get back to the biblical standard. That means that you start with yourself and God. That means that you then move out to your family. Beyond that, the church steps in. And before the church does anything, it confronts that child who is now grown and is not taking care of a mother who is alone.

If the church does for a widow what a grown child is called to do and takes the responsibility off of him or her, we are doing just what the government does: helping him or her to be irresponsible. I'm not saying that you let a widow go without help just because her children are irresponsible. But what I am saying is that we have to get hold of this thing and start bringing our actions in line with God's will.

When people in a family are functioning the way they should toward a single parent or widow, then the church can use its reserves for the people who really need it because they have no one else. Then that frees the government up to take care of what the government needs to take care of—that is, giving us a peaceful, well-ordered, and just society to live in. The government cannot spend its time maintaining peace and order if it has to have bureaucrats monitoring massive welfare programs. It has to put out billions of dollars toward welfare programs that could be going to safety and protection and well-being in society.

The way around this for the future is for men to make sure that, as long as they are alive, their family won't be a single-parent family. We can't solve all the problems of the existing single-parent families, but we can prevent the problem for those who have families now. This means that men are going to have to rise up and carry the standard as kingdom men. We are going to have to hold high God's standard and be men of godly commitment and integrity. We have a generation of emasculated males. They wear pants, but that's the only way you know they are men. They are not willing to step up to the plate. They are not willing to take care of the children they are responsible for.

We need to teach our sons to be responsible so that the next generation does not inherit the heartbreak and curse of shattered families, so that little boys won't have to ask their pastors, "Why won't God answer my prayer and give me a dad?"

I'm reminded of the little boy whose father was on a business trip. As he was sitting in his father's chair, his older sister got upset because she didn't want to see her little brother trying to act so big. She wanted to embarrass him, so she said, "How much is seven plus seven?"

The little guy thought for a moment and answered, "I'm busy. Go ask your mother."

That's the image many kids have of their father. We fathers are going to have to stop being so distracted if we are going to reverse this growing trend toward single-parent families.

I want to tell you what I tell the single parents in my church. We love you and care about you. We know we are only one heartbeat away from being single parents ourselves. I also want to say I know it's not easy, but we have to do things God's way if we want His blessing.

By way of review, that means you start with your personal responsibility. Then you go to your extended family. If no one is there, you appeal to the church. And, as a last resort, you go to the government. Whereas one circle can support the other, it cannot and should not replace it, for each must bear his own load (Galatians 6:5). When you do it God's way, you experience God's blessings.

YOU ARE NOT ALONE

Even if you're a parent alone, you are not out there alone. God says that if you give yourself to Him He will never leave you or forsake you. Though everyone else may turn away from you, you will never be alone. That doesn't mean you don't have responsibility, but not you, your family, the church, or the government can replace God in your life.

But you may have some practical questions: "How long do I have to be a single parent? How long do I have to wait for a break in my circumstances? How long do I have to wait for someone to share my life with? How long?"

Obviously, I can't answer that. But let me share something God continues to teach me. I fly a lot, and sometimes the plane I'm on gets stuck in a holding pattern. We have to circle the airport for minutes or even hours. You may have been there yourself. On one flight we circled the airport for three hours because of a low cloud cover that had the airport fogged in. It would have been too dangerous to try to land. So the air traffic controller said we had to stay up.

You know, I could not see any of the problems they

were talking about because I was at 30,000 feet. The problems were at 500 to 1,000 feet. All I could see was clear skies.

But the pilot knew something I did not know. There was danger below. The pilot was in contact with somebody I could not see or hear, the air traffic controller in the tower. These people said it was too dangerous to land.

Of course, the other passengers and I were fidgeting and getting tired and frustrated because we had places to go and people to see and things to do. But the pilot said we had to keep circling until the tower said it was safe to come down.

> GOD KNOWS HOW TO GET YOU FROM WHERE YOU ARE TO WHERE HE WANTS YOU TO BE.

My friend if you feel like you're in a holding pattern going nowhere, don't come down too soon. You may be heading straight down into a low cloud cover that will obscure your landing. If you try to land on your own before God brings you in, you might crash and be far worse off than you were in that holding pattern.

I understand that single parenthood can feel like a perpetual holding pattern that's getting you nowhere. It may be that God has you up in the air right now, but I can tell you this. As long as you need to fly, there will be enough fuel in the plane. For as long as God keeps you up there, there will be enough to keep you going.

If you are about to run out of fuel, God may take you

to a different airport to land. He may want to take you somewhere entirely new, but let Him set the flight pattern. He has flown this way before. He has been on this flight many times.

God knows how to get you from where you are to where He wants you to be. So when you begin to get tired while you're waiting on God, do what a lot of airline passengers do. Go to sleep. Sit back and rest in God's love. Let Him take care of the stuff you can't fix. He knows exactly where He's taking you, and He will most certainly give you a safe landing.

God bless you as you walk in His will and discover the fullness of His love for you.

THE URBAN ALTERNATIVE
The National Ministry of Dr. Tony Evans

Dr. Tony Evans and The Urban Alternative (TUA) **equips, empowers,** and **unites** Christians to **impact** *individuals, families, churches,* and *communities* to restore hope and transform lives.

We believe the core cause of the problems we face in our personal lives, homes, churches, and societies is a spiritual one; therefore, the only way to address them is spiritually. We've tried a political, a social, an economic, and even a religious agenda. It's time for a Kingdom Agenda—God's visible and comprehensive rule over every area of life, because when we function as we were designed, there is a divine power that changes everything. It renews and restores as the life of Christ is made manifest within our own. As we align ourselves under Him, there is an alignment that happens from deep within—where He brings about full restoration. It is an atmosphere that revives and makes whole.

As it impacts us, it impacts others—transforming every sphere of life in which we live. When each biblical sphere of life functions in accordance with God's Word, the outcomes are evangelism, discipleship, and community impact. As we learn how to govern ourselves under God, we then transform the institutions of family, church, and society from a biblically based kingdom perspective where, through Him, we are touching heaven and changing earth.

To achieve our goal we use a variety of strategies, methods, and resources for reaching and equipping as many people as possible.

Broadcast Media

Hundreds of thousands of individuals experience *The Alternative with Dr. Tony Evans* through the daily radio broadcast playing on nearly **1,000 radio outlets** and in over **130 countries**. The broadcast can also be seen on several television networks, and is viewable online at TonyEvans.org.

Leadership Training

The Kingdom Agenda Pastors (KAP) provides a *viable network* for *like-minded pastors* who embrace the Kingdom

Agenda philosophy. Pastors have the opportunity to go deeper with Dr. Tony Evans as they are given greater biblical knowledge, practical applications, and resources to impact individuals, families, churches, and communities. KAP welcomes *senior and associate pastors* of all churches.

The Kingdom Agenda Pastors' Summit develops church leaders to meet the demands of the twenty-first century while maintaining the Gospel message and the strategic position of the church. The Summit introduces *intensive seminars, workshops,* and *resources,* addressing issues affecting the community, family, leadership, organizational health, and more.

Pastors' Wives Ministry, founded by Dr. Lois Evans, provides *counsel, encouragement,* and *spiritual resources* for pastors' wives as they serve with their husbands in the ministry. A primary focus of the ministry is the KAP Summit that offers senior pastors' wives a safe place to *reflect, renew,* and *relax* along with training in personal development, spiritual growth, and care for their emotional and physical well-being.

COMMUNITY IMPACT

National Church Adopt-A-School Initiative (NCAASI) prepares churches across the country to impact communities by using *public schools as the primary vehicle for effecting positive social change* in urban youth and families. Leaders of churches, school districts, faith-based organizations, and other nonprofit organizations are equipped with the knowledge and tools to *forge partnerships* and build *strong social service delivery systems*. This training is based on the comprehensive church-based community impact strategy conducted by Oak Cliff Bible Fellowship. It addresses such areas as economic development, education, housing, health revitalization, family renewal, and racial reconciliation. We also assist churches in tailoring the model to meet the specific needs of their communities while simultaneously addressing the spiritual and moral frame of reference.

RESOURCE DEVELOPMENT

We are fostering lifelong learning partnerships with the people we serve by providing a variety of published materials. We offer booklets, Bible studies, books, CDs, and DVDs to strengthen people in their walk with God and ministry to others.

* * *

For more information, a catalog of Dr. Tony Evans' ministry resources, and a complimentary copy of Dr. Evans' devotional newsletter, call (800) 800-3222 or write TUA at P.O. Box 4000, Dallas TX 75208, or log on to www.TonyEvans.org

EVANS
THE URBAN ALTERNATIVE

At The Urban Alternative, the national ministry of Dr. Tony Evans, we seek to restore hope and transform lives to reflect the values of the kingdom of God. Along with our community outreach initiative, leadership training and family and personal growth emphasis, Dr. Evans continues to minister to people from the pulpit to the heart as the relevant expositor with the powerful voice. Lives are touched both locally and abroad through our daily radio broadcast, weekly television ministry and internet access points.

PRESENTING AN
ALTERNATIVE TO:

COMMUNITY OUTREACH

Equipping leaders to engage public schools and communities with mentoring, family support services and a commitment to a brighter tomorrow.

LEADERSHIP TRAINING

Offering an exclusive opportunity for pastors and their wives to receive discipleship from Drs. Tony and Lois Evans and the TUA staff, along with networking opportunities, resources and encouragement.

FAMILY AND PERSONAL GROWTH

Strengthening homes and deepening spiritual lives through helpful resources that encourage hope and health for the glory of God.

TONYEVANS.ORG

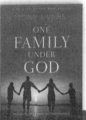
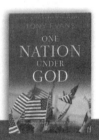